Contents

Executive summary

When attempting breakthrough innovation, the established firm is its own worst enemy. Numerous barriers within the firm inhibit its employees and their attempts at innovation. These include organisational inertia, cultural resistance, an aversion to risk, insufficient or inappropriate incentives and an overcommitment to existing customers. Yet despite these barriers, our research has shown that there are ways that established firms can organise for breakthrough innovation.

Survey research undertaken as part of this project indicates that there are four ways in particular by which firms can help to create an entrepreneurial environment and make significant improvements to supporting breakthrough innovation projects:

- encouraging greater risk-taking

- accepting that failure of some radical innovation projects is a natural part of the learning process

- making it is easy to achieve organisational buy-in

- developing innovation incentive programmes that give employees ownership of radical projects

The focus of innovative activities can be on the identification and development of new ideas and technologies to the demonstration stage (exploration), or the commercialisation of technologies and intellectual property that have already been demonstrated (exploitation).

These activities can be viewed as being driven from the bottom-up, by the actions of entrepreneurially-minded individuals (intrapreneurs), or from the top-down through senior management initiatives (corporate entrepreneurship). This report provides case examples of both these approaches from ARM, Philips, BT, Qualcomm and BAE Systems. These demonstrate how linking the four elements identified above improves a firm's capacity to generate breakthrough innovations.

Introduction

Conventional wisdom would have us believe that new entrepreneurial firms are the source of radical innovation and that large established firms are only successful at making incremental improvements to existing products. Yet the development of a diverse range of revolutionary products, such as the Intel microprocessor, Johnson Matthey's catalytic converter, the VHS video cassette recorder and the Apple iPod is testament to the fact that established firms can achieve breakthrough innovations which sustain their competitiveness in existing markets and create advantages in new ones.

Established, technology-based firms recognise the imperative to innovate, with the majority having specialist R&D units specifically to promote technological innovation. However, the strength of these R&D units has traditionally been in their ability to innovate incrementally, in the development of modifications and refinements to existing products and processes, rather than in their ability to generate radical innovations. This behaviour derives from the fact that such firms have too many obligations, and too much to lose, to justify the risks of chasing radical possibilities whose success is so uncertain.

This report provides a number of explanations as to why these behaviours arise before going on to suggest some approaches which firms can use to improve their capacity to generate breakthrough innovations.

The iPod and iTunes store revolutionised Apple, developing market leadership in music downloads
Image: Apple Inc.

Innovation: incremental, radical and breakthrough

Innovation is the generation and commercialisation of novel ideas, products, processes and services. A wide variety of terminologies has been used to describe different types of innovation. Innovations can be classed as being either *incremental* or *radical*, according to their degree of technological novelty. Innovations can also be categorised according to whether the target market is one in which the firm already competes, or is one in which it is entering for the first time.

Incremental innovations are critical to sustaining a firm's share in mainstream markets. They focus on improving existing products and services to satisfy ever-changing customer demands. They usually emphasise cost or feature improvements to existing products or services.

By contrast, radical innovation concerns the development of new businesses or product lines based on new ideas or technologies. Radical innovations produce substantial performance improvements or cost reductions that significantly alter the consumption patterns of a market.

Breakthrough innovations establish a new degree of competitiveness in either an existing or a new market. The technology behind such innovations may be radical – or may be an incremental development if the firm is entering a new market (see Figure 1 overleaf).

Research approach

A case study approach was followed for this project in order to try to understand the processes through which breakthrough innovations are developed and the characteristics of those firms that develop them.

Data collected from these qualitative case studies of technology-based firms was complemented by a survey that was conducted during the winter of 2008/9. This survey was used to explore the links between intrapreneurship and breakthrough innovation and was completed by 64 individuals with a responsibility for making technology management decisions in large UK technology-based firms.

The evidence from these case studies and the survey underpin the guidelines presented in this report.

The robotic kit Mindstorms opened up new markets for Lego.
Image: LEGO Group

Market

Technology		Existing	New
	Incremental	Sustaining	**Breakthrough**
	Radical	**Breakthrough**	**Breakthrough**

Figure 1. Modes of breakthrough innovation

Barriers to breakthrough innovation in established firms

Organisational inertia

Cultural resistance

Lack of incentives and aversion to risk

Overcommitment to current customers

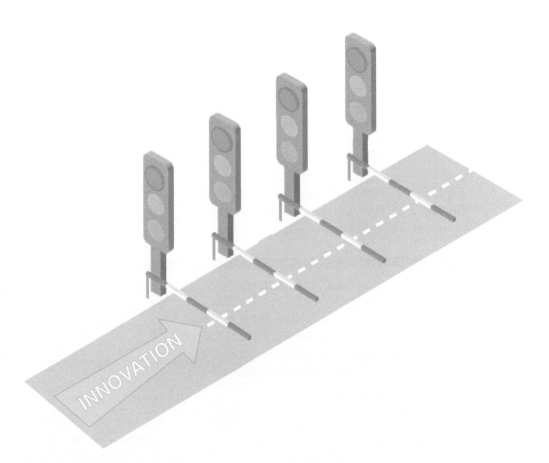

INNOVATION

Organisational inertia

Organisational inertia refers to the role that structured routines play in constraining the actions of incumbent firms and their ability to compete successfully. Organisations develop highly structured routines in order to reduce the costs associated with information acquisition and coordination. Establishing such efficient routines is crucial for organisational learning and performance. However, over time these routines may hinder the ability of the firm to adapt; the structures and systems that facilitate survival in stable and predictable environments become liabilities in environments undergoing rapid change.

Furthermore, an increasing reliance on efficient routines may prevent firms from sensing valuable opportunities that would drag them beyond those practices. Organisational evolution and learning research suggests that, as organisational routines become entrenched, organisations tend to exploit existing knowledge and capabilities, possibly crowding out more exploratory activities.

The inability to recognise the value of new information, assimilate it, and apply it to commercial ends has been described as a reason why incumbent firms have difficulties reacting to breakthrough innovations. It arises from limitations in what is termed the firm's 'absorptive capacity'. Such capacity is built incrementally upon prior and related knowledge. Radical innovations however, generally require knowledge that exists outside the firm and incumbents are often unable to recognise and fully embrace new technological paradigms.

Cultural resistance

As successful organisations become larger and older they tend to develop shared expectations about how things are done, leading to a cultural resistance to change. Problems arise because cultural inertia is ephemeral and difficult to address directly. Consequently, management often fails to introduce change even when they recognise its necessity.

This problem is exacerbated by the tendency of organisational departments to develop their own ways of viewing the world, which can inhibit the kind of collective action that is necessary for innovation. Shared orientations reflect the identity of the departments; members create these identities on the basis of things they know how to do well. Furthermore, deviating from existing knowledge domains also poses a threat to the identity of the organisation.

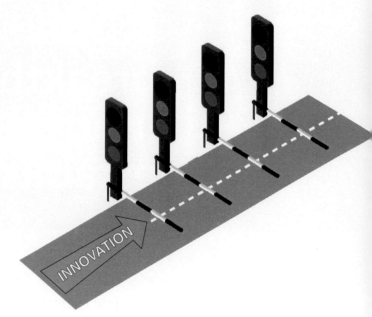

Lack of incentives and aversion to risk

While there are clear benefits to proactive change, only a small minority of farsighted firms initiate discontinuous change before a performance decline. Part of this stems from the risks involved in proactive change. Large corporations are comfortable developing sustaining technologies, which build on their existing strengths, because radical new technologies may destabilise their core competencies. Established firms excel at knowing their markets and having mechanisms in place to improve existing technologies. Yet innovating in this way has the potential to reduce technical variation and stunt a firm's learning potential.

Radical technologies often look financially unattractive or excessively risky to incumbents. Many of these higher risk initiatives can only be developed over a considerable period of time; in pharmaceutical and aerospace industries this can sometimes be as long as 20 years. The time-horizon required to build up knowledge about potential markets, and to develop the technologies involved, is much longer than with incremental innovations.

The potential market for these radical technologies may initially appear small, attracting low revenues, with the newness of the market making it difficult to determine the most likely customers and their actual needs. As a result, it is not uncommon that hundreds of new ideas get killed before any one innovation successfully reaches the market.

Furthermore, there is a need for more 'patient money' to be invested. In a corporate world where shareholders pay close attention to quarterly reports, the need for quick results frequently reduces the patience required for breakthroughs.

As a result of these factors there are limited incentives for major companies to invest in breakthrough innovations and it is unusual for them to re-invent themselves in order to develop dramatically new business models.

Overcommitment to current customers

Market orientation endorses the classic marketing principle that firms should stay close to their customers and prioritise the needs of those they currently serve. However, in recent years doubts have been raised regarding the unquestioning emphasis that firms place on these markets. It is possible that too great a focus on existing customers could lead to trivial innovations and myopic R&D, which in turn may reduce the firm's innovative capability.

Major innovations display a very different package of attributes from those that mainstream customers historically value. It is very difficult for companies to predict accurately which attributes of a radical technology a consumer will find valuable. Operating under such uncertainty, a customer-oriented firm continues to serve its existing market, pursuing those innovations that directly address existing customers' unsatisfied needs and that promise the best short-term returns. As a consequence, it dedicates fewer resources to market-based innovations that have an unknown future, stifling the generation of radical innovations.

Listening too closely to the current wants of their existing customer base can therefore lead companies to fail to spot the true market potential for breakthrough technologies and miss emerging technological opportunities.

> *"A radical innovation would be a complete departure from our current product type. The company tends to have a 'production' mentality working to do what we are already doing but more efficiently. However, we recognise the need for innovation in order to grow the business, but in our case this would very probably be incremental."*
> **Strategic Technology Manager, manufacturing firm**

> *"There is little appetite in the current climate to spend on R&D. The company is not 'cash rich' and any spend is almost an 'Act of Parliament' to move forward, slowing pace right down. Tax rebates are far too slow to have incentive as many firms need the cash back straight away, not in 18 months to 2 years."*
> **Head of R&D, construction firm**

Overcoming the innovation barrier

Two challenges for established firms

Enabling conditions

Creating an entrepreneurial environment

Supporting the emergence of promising ideas and technologies

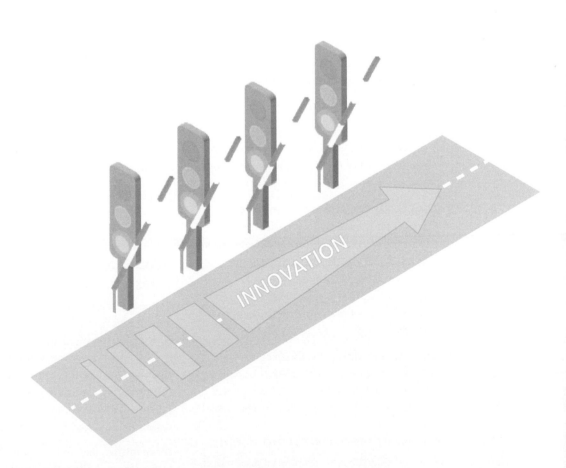

Two challenges for established firms

The danger of being deposed by upstart market newcomers and incumbents in other markets means that established firms face two concurrent challenges:

- remaining competitive in the short-term through the exploitation of existing lines of business and incremental innovation

- simultaneously developing breakthrough innovations that allow the firm to make significant advances in existing markets or to enter new ones

However, as the issues discussed in the previous section indicate, the dominant practices and routines that support success in one market may represent significant barriers to the development of breakthrough innovations.

So, how can established firms develop breakthrough innovations to sustain or transform their competitiveness?

Enabling conditions

Although the history of breakthrough innovations is populated with examples of serendipity and unpredictability, research indicates that two fundamental enabling conditions are necessary for established firms to successfully pursue breakthrough innovation:

- the firm must create an environment conducive to idea generation

- the firm must have the fortitude and risk tolerance to persevere, and to allow the most promising ideas and technologies to emerge

The first enabling condition is the upstream creative challenge of developing the ability to 'see differently'. Since radical concepts often spring from the imagination of individuals or teams, the challenge is to create an organisational context where creativity can flourish. The second enabling condition is the downstream implementation challenge of matching the concept to actual market needs.

Without the ability to see differently, the firm is unable to change the rules of the game; while without the ability to implement it, the firm will join the ranks of companies that failed to capitalise on their pioneering inventions.

Creating an entrepreneurial environment

It has been observed that the entrepreneurial orientation of a firm has a significant effect on the development of radical innovations. Results from a survey conducted at the Centre for Technology Management indicate that this is one which comprises the following:

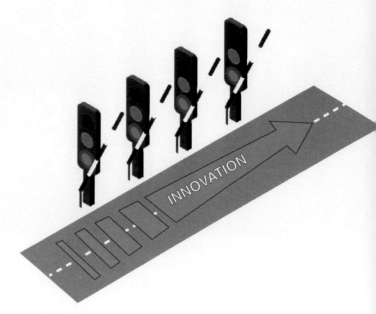

An entrepreneurial environment: a culture in the firm which encourages everyone to take part in innovation.

An environment where all ideas are welcome: employees are encouraged to come forward with ideas, even if they have only a vague idea of the potential market applications for the idea.

Acceptance of failure in radical innovation projects: failure in radical innovation projects is accepted within the firm and considered a natural part of the learning process.

Hunting for new ideas: technical people with business development skills are tasked with finding new sources of potential radical ideas within the firm, moving ideas forward in the innovation process through preparation of business cases.

Celebrating and respecting success: successful innovators of breakthrough ideas are celebrated and respected within the firm, serving as inspiration for others.

Supporting the emergence of promising ideas and technologies

While the creation of a more entrepreneurial environment contributes towards a cultural change in the organisation, project management approaches can also support the development of radical innovations. It has been suggested that there should be a core group of people who have the responsibility for driving radical innovation, as dedicated personnel and funding are required to achieve the best results and maintain accountability.

Mechanisms need to be put in place that support those with ideas and allow these ideas to be brought forward. Three types of opportunity recognisers have been identified that enhance the organisation's capacity for the development of radical innovations: gatherers, hunters and radical innovation hubs. Gatherers and hunters are passive and active opportunity recognisers respectively, while a radical innovation hub is an organisational repository for capturing and evaluating ideas.

Firms should attempt to remove barriers that get in the way of entrepreneurial-minded individuals and should try to align personal and organisational initiatives more closely. Results from the survey show that the greatest scope for improvement lies in improving the opportunity for employees to become 'owners' of radical innovation projects. This can be achieved by offering equity options or by investing part of their yearly bonus. Such approaches mean that individuals share some of the potential risks of a radical innovation project and provide them with greater personal incentives to succeed.

Senior management support is also a critical factor in the early product development process. This organisational support is necessary for obtaining the funding, resources and personnel required for successful development. The survey revealed that there is a need for improved mechanisms to support such organisational buy-in.

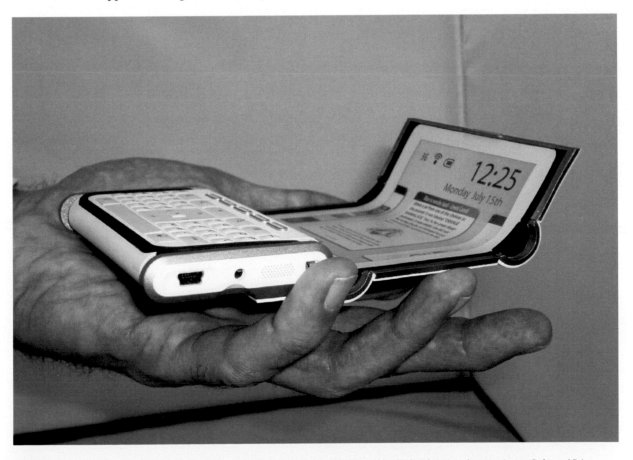

The long development time required for breakthrough innovations such as those by Philips Technology Incubator spin-out Polymer Vision highlights the need for patience from senior management (see case study page 22).

Image: Polymer Vision

Intrapreneurship

Entrepreneurial individuals

Case study

ARM: Integrating the intrapreneur

BOTTOM-UP & EMERGENT

Entrepreneurial individuals

Successful breakthrough innovation would not occur without the actions of individuals who have a passion for and belief in the innovation. The emergence of radical innovations in established firms is driven by these entrepreneurial individuals, known as 'intrapreneurs'. Intrapreneurship is the act or practice of creating new products and business opportunities within an organisation by empowering employees to be more creative and risk-taking in their work. As a bottom-up, emergent, employee-driven practice, it contrasts with the top-down structure that corporate entrepreneurship employs (see next section).

Rather than simply relying on organisational systems to manage the innovation process, the challenge for the organisation is to harness the energy and passion of these intrapreneurs. The internal systems of firms often inhibit intrapreneurial activity and there are cultural, cognitive and structural barriers that intrapreneurs must overcome if they are to succeed.

Evidence from prior research indicates that some degree of hierarchical flexibility is necessary to promote intrapreneurship and support intrapreneurs within the organisation as inflexibility can inhibit individual action. These intrapreneurs need funds and resources if they are to explore novel and pioneering technologies, with this pursuit requiring considerable slack resources. Furthermore, individuals often need guidance and emotional support in order to be able to act in an intrapreneurial fashion. This may involve practical coaching, together with personal counselling and mentoring support.

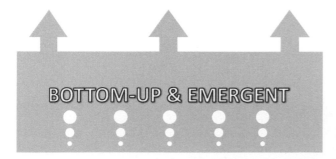

BOTTOM-UP & EMERGENT

CASE STUDY

ARM: Integrating the intrapreneur

The mbed project was informally initiated by an ARM engineer, Chris Styles, who saw the opportunity for the development of a standard microcontroller device for educational applications in schools. He found a colleague in ARM, Simon Ford, who was equally enthusiastic and together they began to prototype a PC-controlled microcontroller platform that they called "mbed". During the next 18 months the pair used whatever ARM resources were available to them in their spare time. They presented and demonstrated their work-in-progress to their colleagues and senior management. While they found some support much of the time they met indifference, resistance and even hostility to what they were doing.

As they made progress, however, these negative reactions to the mbed project began to dissipate. Demonstrating their prototype to senior management led to the CTO approving a budget for a formal product development process. This allowed the team funds to subcontract some of the necessary work outside ARM and to make more rapid progress. Having successfully passed through the product development stage gates, the first sales deal was clinched in January 2009.

While the project ultimately proved successful, Chris and Simon needed to work very hard as intrapreneurs. They were frequently working against the organisation and early approaches to senior management and colleagues were met with strong resistance. A great deal of persistence and belief in the value of the project was required to succeed. It was important that during the formative, informal stages of the project that they each had a peer supporter on whom they could depend and to whom they were able to voice their frustrations.

Critical to gaining organisational support was that – as a project engineer in ARM's R&D division – Simon Ford had been involved in the development of leading edge microprocessors for mobile devices for over 6 years before he began to champion, mbed. During this time he had worked closely with the CTO and developed a reputation as someone who could "get things done". As disagreements come with the territory of trying to do something different, the project members often needed to be protected so that they felt safe to experiment. Once the project was formally recognised, Chris and Simon had their own office where they gained this protected space and could work uninterrupted from the distractions of other projects. It also provided a location where subcontractors could visit and continue the development work. This use of external resources is a common feature of intrapreneurial individuals and very different to the usual corporate approach. Bureaucracy is circumvented and established practices ignored so that activities can be completed more quickly and with less expense.

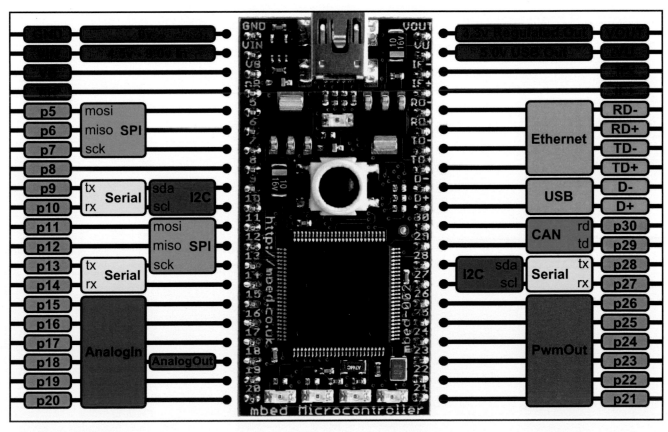

The mbed microcontroller.
Image: Arm Holdings

Corporate entrepreneurship

Top-down approach

Corporate incubators

Case study

Philips: bringing the market into the organisation

TOP-DOWN & STRUCTURED

Top-down approach

In an attempt to create an environment conducive to breakthrough innovation, established firms have turned to corporate entrepreneurship. Corporate entrepreneurship is a process by which a firm searches for and exploits the entrepreneurial opportunities that arise from the technological or market knowledge it already possesses. The result of these activities is the creation of a new business that is distinct from the parent company. It is a top-down approach led by senior management with the aim of stimulating the development and commercialisation of new opportunities. While there are a number of corporate entrepreneurship approaches that can be implemented, we have observed one model that stands out as being effective in large technology-based firms: corporate incubators.

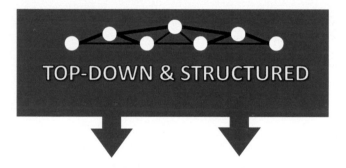

TOP-DOWN & STRUCTURED

Corporate incubators

Corporate incubators are specialised corporate units that draw on the organisation's resources to support the development of new ventures. The primary purpose of incubators is to provide a supportive environment for new ventures in which they are protected from external pressures until they are ready. There are a number of features common to the majority of incubators:

- shared office space and support services

- professional business support

- internal or external network provision

Corporate incubators are set up to either explore or to exploit business opportunities – sometimes both of these. Explorative incubators invest in opportunities that arise inside the parent firm and actively nurture and develop these so that, over time, they became sources of growth for the firm.

Incubators established to exploit opportunities try to capitalise on the parent firm's existing assets (such as patents, technologies, raw ideas and managerial talent).

The case of Philips and its technology incubator provides a good example of how long-term initiatives can be successful if they have consistent board-level support and create selection pressures similar to those found in the market.

CASE STUDY

Philips: Bringing the market into the organisation

While the majority of corporate incubators are jettisoned before they bear fruit, the Philips Technology Incubator has proved successful in terms of both its longevity (it has been operational since 2001), for steadily spinning out new ventures and for spawning two new incubators. The incubator was formed following the recognition by the new CTO, Ad Huijser, that technological innovation should be at the forefront of Philips' activities but that long-term breakthrough projects needed to be protected from the pressures of immediate revenue generation.

The incubator programme was initiated with the aim of nurturing ideas developed in the company's research departments that would otherwise be lost but which had potential long-term strategic value to Philips. The incubator was led by an experienced Philips man, Jelto Smits. He set the criteria by which venture teams would be allowed to enter the incubator. The potential ventures needed to demonstrate that the intellectual property governing the technology was protectable; the technology had the potential to create a market worth €100 million or more; the technology would have a disruptive effect on the market it was entering; the venture's technology was strategically aligned with Philips' long-term corporate strategy; and the team was both motivated and capable.

Subject to meeting these criteria, venture teams were accepted and provided with funds, an operational base at the High Tech Campus in Eindhoven and business support. The first ventures admitted to the incubator were subject to an informal review process but later ventures were guided by a formal stage gate process (the Bell-Mason framework). This allowed both the incubator management team and the venture teams to better understand the maturity of the technology and its market readiness.

As the technologies developed by the venture teams reached maturity they were reviewed to determine whether they were still aligned with Philips' corporate strategy. Those technologies that still met this criteria were integrated into one of the firm's operating divisions, while those that were determined to no longer do so were spun-out through a partnership with the venturing firm, New Venture Partners. By 2005, Philips had enhanced its technical competences through the integration of two novel technologies into its operating divisions, while three others had been spun-out. Recognising then that some of the best ideas within the research division had already been mined by the incubator, Huijser then initiated the creation of two new incubators in January 2006 in domains into which Philips intended to move: lifestyle technologies and medical instrumentation. In contrast to the first technology incubator, these new incubators were market-oriented; venture teams that had recognised market opportunities or problems were admitted into the incubators, allowing the teams to search for potential technical solutions both within Philips and beyond.

The Philips case shows how the incubator as internal explorer has led to the development of technical competences that would otherwise have been eliminated if they had remained in the corporate research laboratories. That it has to date proven successful may be attributed to a number of factors, most significantly the role that Huijser played as a Board-level champion. As he anticipated, the purpose of the incubator was questioned after only a single year of its existence, but with his support it was protected through the vagaries of the business cycle. The fact that the incubator CEO, Jelto Smits, had over twenty years of experience in a variety of technical, commercial and legal roles at Philips helped to ensure that there was continuity in the selection process and in the strategic alignment of the technologies being developed in the incubator.

Philips acknowledged the need to diversify its approach to the acquisition of technical competences with its introduction of two new incubators. While the firm has begun to acquire technical competences internally, it recognises that such competences also exist beyond the boundary of the firm.

Although the incubator has established processes to support the development of new technologies, the main difficulty for Philips remains at the end of the process. Those technologies that are strategically aligned with the firm, need to be introduced into the operating divisions. This can be a significant challenge as the divisions often fiercely resist the introduction of new technologies. This resistance stems from political concerns and worries that the new technology could displace existing ones. For technologies that are not strategically aligned, such as those developed in the incubator by Polymer Vision, Silicon Hive and Handshake Solutions, a spin-out of the venture is the appropriate commercialisation route.

Philips Laser Sensors was successfully transferred from the Technology Incubator to the Sector Lighting Division.

Image: Twin-Eye Laser™ sensor © Philips

Integrating approaches for breakthrough innovation

Combining approaches

Selecting the best ideas

Organisational structures

Case studies

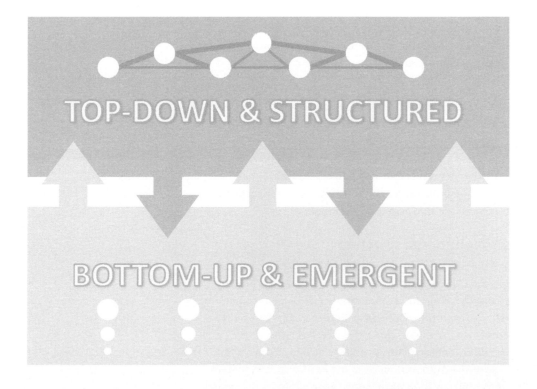

Combining approaches

To achieve successful breakthrough innovation there is a need to combine both of the approaches outlined in the previous sections: 'top-down' organisational structures that are linked to business objectives, with new ideas and technologies emerging through 'bottom-up' intrapreneurial activity. To attempt one without the other is to severely limit the potential occurrence of breakthroughs.

While there are potential intrapreneurs in all firms, the degree to which they are given the freedom and resources necessary to build up their novel concepts (ie 'slack time') affects their ability to develop these concepts to a stage where their value is recognised by senior decision makers.

Persistence is a hallmark of intrapreneurs, both when searching for solutions to the technological problems that arise during development, and in attempting to sell the concept to the organisation and achieve buy-in.

Selecting the best ideas

There needs to be selection processes within the firm that allocate resources to the intrapreneurs with the most promising ideas and technologies. Without these selection processes, intrapreneurial activity can lack direction and fail to align with the strategic objectives of the firm. The latter famously occurred at Xerox in the 1970s when a number of radically new technologies were invented but were not commercialised because Xerox had identified itself as a copier business.

One strategy employed by P&G to overcome this lack of direction is to make the proviso that all new products must fit within an established brand identity. The cost of launching a new brand is prohibitively expensive but the portfolio of brands that P&G possesses means that there remains significant scope for intrapreneurs to make the business case for further development.

Organisational structures

We have shown how a technology incubator can act as an organisational structure to help these selection processes to occur. Using this exploitation strategy in combination with an exploratory phase, as in the case of the BT corporate incubator, can prove effective. Alternative organisational structures can also be adopted, as in the case of the Autonomous Systems Facility at BAE Systems. The emphasis is on harnessing the intrapreneurial capital that a firm possesses and providing a management structure in which it is able to explore the potential of new concepts. These initiatives need to be treated differently as

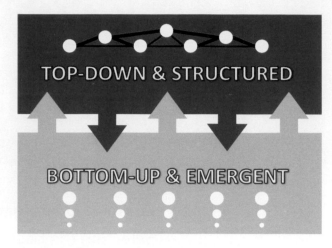

they develop their own identity. They often need separate workspace and resources, with senior management support necessary to protect them from short-term business pressures.

There are other routes by which breakthrough innovations can be achieved. As described in the report "How to implement open innovation,[1]" there are numerous potential sources of knowledge and technology existing outside the boundary of the company which could be acquired to enable innovation. The approaches can be combined with those described in this report. Acquired technologies will often be at an early stage of development, however, and may require further work before they can be commercialised and the kind of approaches described here employed.

There is no single way to achieve breakthrough innovation. It is dependent on a multitude of factors, including the size and maturity of the firm, the industry in which it operates and its position within it, the type of people the firm employs, and the technological resource base of the firm. What works for one firm, therefore, may not be the most appropriate approach for another.

[1] Mortara, L., Napp, J.J., Slacik, I., Minshall, T.W. (2009). *How to implement open innovation: Lessons from studying large multinational companies.* Institute for Manufacturing, University of Cambridge.

CASE STUDY

BT: Exploring and exploiting the idea space

BT set up its corporate incubator, Brightstar, in 2000. It did so because it recognised its ongoing failure to exploit its vast portfolio of 14,000 patents, to which it was adding as many as 300 new ones each year. The objective of the incubator was to develop this intellectual property and launch new ventures worth £100 million or more.

While BT's ultimate objective was the exploitation of its intellectual property base, its internal processes needed to be exploratory in nature at first as the incubator management sought to identify and foster projects around this IP. The incubator team sought to do this and to 'create a buzz' through a series of drop-in sessions. It was at these sessions that BT scientists and engineers could freely discuss their ideas with the incubator management. The Brightstar team was conscious of the nervousness of the researchers at these sessions and made it clear that there were no bad ideas.

The BT incubator management met potential intrapreneurs during drop-in sessions, at which management would make suggestions to the ideas that were put forward, guiding their creators through the early concept stages as they devised their business plans. External partners were brought in to form an advisory panel and provide expertise in the selection of the nascent projects. Those that passed the judgement of the panel were then admitted to the incubator, where they received funding and access to BT resources. This structured approach, supported with management and marketing functions, ensured that intrapreneurs with promising ideas could receive the resources necessary to develop their technologies to commercial readiness.

While the incubator successfully launched a number of profitable ventures, it did so at a time of financial upheaval in the telecommunications sector. Cost-cutting measures meant that despite the incubation and spin-out costs of these ventures being miniscule in comparison to the multi-billion pound acquisitions that it was making, BT decided to cease funding the incubator after less than three years of operation. A lack of patience meant that a number of promising BT technologies didn't reach commercial readiness as they were stuck in development limbo. However, despite this turmoil, a number of the ventures that were successful spun-out have since been contracted by BT to provide the novel technologies they have successfully developed. This spin-out mode represents another mode through which breakthrough innovation can be achieved.

CASE STUDY

Qualcomm: Harnessing the power of employee involvement to drive breakthrough innovation

When in 2006, mobile technologies firm Qualcomm decided to invest further in breakthrough innovations to complement its core wireless business, it turned to its employees for ideas. It soon realized that there were three central challenges in increasing employee involvement in breakthrough innovation: (1) The generation and capture of a large number of ideas (2) the efficient selection of the most promising ideas and (3) the accompanying execution of new ideas within an organisation focused on existing customer commitments.

Ricardo dos Santos, a Senior Director of Business Development at Qualcomm corporate was tasked with devising a systematic and sustainable approach to these central challenges. Ricardo turned to a proven method conspicuously absent in the corporate world – idea contests, such as university business plan competitions or non-profit organisation challenges such as the X Prize.

Ricardo setup the Qualcomm VentureFest in 2006 as a year-round employee idea tournament. It provided a call for innovation from the top, establishing clear rules and timelines for participation, and a process for selection and follow-up. To address the first challenge, the generation and capture of a large number of ideas, the VentureFest tournament is supported by an online idea management system to collect ideas in a simple, yet standardised form. In many other competitions, committees of experts are used to select the most promising ideas. However, it was realised that in VentureFest, such a committee could be easily overwhelmed with handling the enormous and diverse set of ideas that would be generated. Instead, peer assessment was identified as an efficient mechanism for idea selection. Accordingly, the online system also contains message boards, rating systems and prediction markets so that all employees, especially self-selected, subject matter experts, could also participate in the decision making process.

Finally, to address the third challenge, execution of new ideas, the VentureFest tournament includes a 'boot camp' phase. Here the shortlisted, most promising ideas are further developed by their employee champions. Executive mentors guide the champions through the discovery and early stage funding process, through to the proper commercialisation platform, spin-in to an internal business unit or corporate incubator, or an external spin-out arrangement.

To date, with four competition cycles completed, the VentureFest has received participation from over one third of the company's employees (roughly 5,000 out of 15,000). Nearly $150 million in internal funding has been secured for the various proposals to be developed past the proof-of-concept stage. It has led to the launch of a half-dozen breakthrough businesses for Qualcomm, including the Zeebo wireless gaming console and the BLUR augmented reality engine for smart devices. The VentureFest is also credited with a marked improvement in employee skills and attitude in relation to corporate entrepreneurship and innovation.

CASE STUDY

BAE Systems: Creating a counter-cultural environment

The origin of BAE Systems' autonomous vehicle capability lies in experiments by some passionate engineers who tested autonomous control systems on model aircraft. This was an 'off the radar' activity that these engineers were pursuing out of office hours while making use of the company resources available to them.

As the group started to make headway, their activities were picked up by senior management. The potential significance of what they were doing was not immediately recognised. Eventually though the company took the decision to formalise the group and to create a facility in which this research could continue.

From these initial intrapreneurial endeavours, the Autonomous Systems Facility was created as a counter-cultural environment in which radical innovation would occur. The approach within the facility is to incrementally innovate at a more rapid pace, with breakthroughs the result of this accumulated effort. The approach taken is based on the idea that creativity often derives from having to overcome adversity; accordingly, engineers are provided with few resources. However, while the facility has a permanent core of employees, it also has the ability to draw on other divisions within the organisation, to second individuals with particular expertise. Working in this way complements the natural tendencies of the intrapreneurs who started the project and it helps maintain a flexible and experimental attitude towards projects.

This approach has worked so far for BAE. The intrapreneurs in the facility are celebrated as heroes and it has received a record number of Chairman's Awards, the internal innovation awards within BAE Systems. By taking this approach BAE believes that it has developed autonomous vehicle capability far more rapidly than it would otherwise have done. And it all started with some engineers playing with model aircraft.

Summary and conclusions

Recommendations for pursuing breakthrough innovation

- **Be patient.** Breakthrough innovation projects often require longer-term resource investments.
- **Remove barriers.** Try to make it easier for intrapreneurial individuals to move forward with their ideas and projects.
- **Provide employee ownership.** Give individuals involved in innovation projects/ventures ownership in them, either through financial incentives or added responsibility.
- **Use stage gate processes.** Monitor the progress of projects and retain only those that remain on track and continue to be strategically attractive.
- **Harness external resources.** It can be quicker and/or cheaper to look outside the organisation for the necessary resources to push a project ahead.

Disruptive technological change is never far away and for established firms it is only a matter of time before the skills and competences they have accumulated are challenged. The successful development and commercialisation of a diverse range of revolutionary products indicates that established firms can achieve breakthrough innovations which sustain their competitiveness in existing markets and create advantages in new markets.

Our research has found that there are new ways of working that help overcome organisational resistance to change and facilitate breakthrough innovation. These practices are either formally designed by senior management (structured) or developed informally and organically through the efforts of intrapreneurs (emergent). The focus may also differ according to whether the aim is to identify ideas and develop new technologies to the demonstration stage (exploration), or to commercialise technologies and intellectual property that have already been demonstrated (exploitation).

Technology incubators are good examples of structured organisational forms as they are the formal creations of senior management. At the turn of the millennium, the Dutch consumer electronics firm Philips established its own incubator. The focus of the Philips Technology Incubator was exploitation. By adopting a set of entry criteria similar to those used by venture capitalists, Philips ensured that the projects entering the incubator were aligned with its strategic objectives and had the potential to become significant revenue generators.

New organisational structures are not only created through senior management initiatives but can also be brought about through the intrapreneurial efforts of individuals within the firm that sequester the resources they need. At semiconductor developer ARM, a pair of engineers brought their CTO an idea for a product outside the usual remit of the firm. Initially rebuffed, they continued to work informally within ARM for almost 18 months before they were able to gain the resources to formally pursue development. During this exploratory phase it was the enthusiasm and drive of these individuals that kept the project alive, along with the support of senior managers who encouraged them not to give up.

The intrapreneurial and corporate approaches need to be combined as it is the integration of intrapreneurial activity with structured selection processes that provides the scope for the firm to achieve breakthrough innovations.

The autonomous vehicles programme at BAE Systems was initially pursued by a group of enthusiastic intrapreneurs who recognised the potential of an autonomous control system that had been developed previously. Seeing the potential applications for the concepts, senior management formalised their work through the creation of the Autonomous Systems Facility (ASF) with further application development ongoing.

The VentureFest competition at Qualcomm created the infrastructure for employees to contribute their ideas and to assess those of others. By using 'the wisdom of the crowd', Qualcomm has been able to improve how it taps into the knowledge and insights that its employees already have, linking their contributions to established business practices to develop breakthrough innovations.

At the telecommunications giant BT, the Brightstar incubator was formed by its CTO in the early 2000s in an attempt to identify and develop latent ideas within the research laboratories. Key to the exploratory mode of operation was the notion that there were no bad ideas and that all ideas were welcome. A structured approach was then added, with venture teams receiving resources in a stage-gated process.

These examples give an idea of what is possible and provide illustrations of how breakthrough innovation can be pursued through new ways of working. There are a variety of ways that firms can approach breakthrough innovation and there is no single way that can be replicated successfully. Firms that are able to repeatedly generate breakthrough innovations are those that provide employees with the resources and space to develop their ideas and side-projects. Such firms also use formal structures and procedures to support the development of breakthrough innovations. For firms looking to explore new areas of business, intrapreneurs must be supported first before any form of formal development occurs. In contrast, for firms attempting to exploit the existing knowledge of the firm, the use of such formal mechanisms helps create an environment conducive to creativity. Balancing the two processes of exploration and exploitation lies at the heart of the innovation process and is the challenge that all firms must address for long term competitiveness.